No Small V

Stories of Hope from the Nativity

by Virginia Wiles

A baby lies crying in a manger. What a strange way for God to deliver the world! Imagine a time of darkness, a time of deep and desperate need. A time when even the least religious pray to God, asking for deliverance. Who among us would imagine that such a rescue would come in infant form? None of our stories include heroes who arrive in diapers, rattle in hand! With the world collapsing in on itself from injustice and violence, why would God not send a full-grown savior?

This God whom we worship works in unconventional ways, surprising the world with new waves of hope. The texts that we will be studying during this unit narrate the familiar story of God's breaking into human history at Christmastime. Most of us have told and acted this story every year for longer than we can remember. No matter how often and how elaborately it is told, the drama of the birth of Jesus keeps coming to us in new meanings, if we are open to new light. We hope that happens in this unit, as we step into the shoes of those who inhabit the nativity stories in the Gospels of Matthew and Luke: Joseph, Mary, Zechariah, Elizabeth, the shepherds, the wisemen, Simeon, and Anna.

Our familiar manger scenes combine the stories of Matthew and Luke, including both the wise men (from Matthew's story) and the shepherds (from Luke's story) in the same scene. Both accounts root the coming of Jesus in the long saga of God's self-revelation through the ages, which was now culminating in salvation on a grand and global scale. The authors of these Gospels clearly knew their Bibles, often quoting or alluding to the Old Testament. For each of them, there was an overarching story: God was doing something unique and new here.

Matthew and Luke's accounts are also each unique. In the Gospel of Matthew the story is told mostly from the perspective of Joseph. Through dreams, Joseph hears God's message and promises, and he responds as a faithful follower. Luke's Gospel focuses more on Mary, the mother of Jesus. The angel Gabriel announces God's message and promises, and Mary submits to the new reality God is birthing.

The narration of both Matthew and Luke make it clear that the birth of Jesus is not an end in itself. His nativity marks the beginning of the fulfillment of God's promises of salvation. It is the preeminent sign of hope for a world that lay "in sin and error pining."

Like the world of first century Palestine, our world is ripe for deliverance. The poor of the Third World, victimized by unfair economic systems, continue to long for justice. North Americans are held in other kinds of captivities, often of their own choosing: consumerism, technology, and various kinds of addictions. Crime on our streets keeps many people living in fear, while more and more people are inhabiting our prisons. Meanwhile, in the small circle of our private lives, each of us can find areas where we long for healing, hope, and fulfillment.

The nativity stories remind us that God wants to renew and save. This year, amidst the noise of Christmas parties and commercials, let us enter the song of the angels: "Peace on earth, good will to all!"

About the Writer
Virginia Wiles is assistant professor of religion at Muhlenberg College, Allentown, Pennsylvania. She is author of the forthcoming book, *Thoughtful Lives: An Introduction to the Thought of the Apostle Paul* (Hendrickson).

Welcome to Good Ground!

Now that you know a little about the topic for this unit, let us introduce you to Good Ground, the series. Good Ground is a unique approach to Bible study. It lets the Bible ask most of the questions and lets participants struggle with the answers. When we ask, "How can I be saved?" the Bible asks, "Whom will you serve?" When we ask, "What will happen to me when I die?" the Bible asks, "What does the Lord require of you?" When we ask, "Whom does God love best?" the Bible asks, "Who is your neighbor?" Good Ground goes to the Scriptures for questions, not just answers.

Here's how each session is structured and what you can expect:

PART I: PREPARATION

We assume that you want to dig into Bible texts enough to do a little reading and thinking between sessions. In this section you are given the Bible passage(s) for the session, a key verse, a summary of the text and the issues it raises, and a three-page study on the text. The section concludes with "Things to think about," which offers some practical applications for everyday living.

We realize that in an age of prepackaged goods and 15-second sound bytes, advance preparation may be a challenge. At the same time, we believe that for God's Word to be relevant to us, we need to do what it takes to ready our hearts and minds.

PART II: SESSION

Here we offer tips for your group when it meets, whether at church, in a home, or in some other setting. Good Ground uses a method for study that begins with everyday life (Focus), moves into an examination of what the Bible says (Engage the Text), then suggests life applications (Respond). The Closing wraps up the study in a brief worship experience.

One of the unique features about Good Ground studies is that they tap into a variety of learning styles. Some people learn best through the traditional lecture and discussion, but many others learn through visuals, imagination, poetry, role-playing and the like. Through these varied learning experiences, Good Ground gets participants involved in the learning, moving beyond the head and into concrete living from the heart.

PART III: LEADER GUIDELINES

We recognize that in many adult groups today, responsibility for leading is passed around within the group—hence the inclusion of notes for the leader in the participant's book. For these sessions to work best, however, those who lead must be prepared ahead of time. This section outlines what materials will be needed for the session, suggests some resources, and offers some tips for making the session come alive. If you are a regular leader of Good Ground, you will likely be aware of our other teaching/leading resources that orient you to our learning philosophy and methods.

Enjoy working with Good Ground as you journey in your faith, growing to be more like Christ!

Julie Garber, editor
Byron Rempel-Burkholder, editor
Ken Hawkley, adult education consultant

Session 1

Accomplice to God's Break~in

PART I: PREPARATION

Bible passage: Matthew 1:1-25

Key verse: "Joseph, son of David, do not fear to take Mary your wife, for that which is conceived in her is of the Holy Spirit; she will bear a son, and you shall call his name Jesus, for he will save his people from their sins." (Matt. 1:20*b*-21 *New Revised Standard Version*)

Summary: Joseph's obedient character allows him to become an active partner with God in God's surprising action to bring salvation in this world. What was Joseph's role in the birth and conception of Jesus? Does God's saving activity need human cooperation?

Study: When we think of the Christmas story we often focus our attention on Mary and the baby Jesus. The great museums of the Western world are filled with paintings and statues of the Mother and Child. The father, meanwhile, seems lost somewhere along the way. Who was Joseph? If Jesus was conceived by the Holy Spirit, was Joseph really necessary? Was he on the scene just to make the holy family seem complete? Does Joseph's presence in our nativity scenes tell us something about who Jesus was?

> The Lord himself will give you a sign. Look, the young woman is with child and shall bear a son, and shall name him Immanuel
>
> —Isaiah 7:14

Matthew starts us off with Joseph and his role in determining the identity of Jesus. Matthew 1 falls into two separate sections: a genealogy of Jesus, and a short narrative about Joseph taking Mary as his wife and naming Mary's child Jesus. Joseph plays a crucial role in both of these sections.

While some people consider genealogies boring and insignificant, they are often one of the things we turn to when we want to determine our identity. Matthew similarly wants to tell us something of who Jesus is by establishing the genealogy of Jesus. He outlines Jesus' ancestry in three sections, each consisting of fourteen generations. This symmetrical organization suggests that God has been consistently and deliberately at work in order to bring about the birth of Jesus.

However, there are also intriguing surprises in the line-up of forebears. In the first section, Matthew includes four of the mothers: Tamar, Rahab, Ruth, and "the wife of Uriah" (Bathsheba). In a patriarchal society, the mention of these female figures is remarkable. Even more remarkable is the fact that each of these women were either Gentile outsiders or they were on the moral fringes of their society:

> *Tamar:* Widow to two sons of Judah, one of the ancestors of the twelve tribes of Israel. When Judah reneged on his promise to marry a third son to her, she disguised herself as a prostitute and Judah himself had intercourse with her, fathering twins. One of the twins, Perez, was ancestor to Jesus.
> *Rahab:* The prostitute who hosted two Israelite spies in Jericho. For her hospitality, God spared her life when Jericho was destroyed, and she was assimilated into the Israelite nation.
> *Ruth:* A Moabite widow of an Israelite whose parents had settled in her region. When her widowed mother-in-law Naomi returns to Canaan, Ruth goes with her. Ruth marries Boaz and becomes the great grandmother of King David.
> *Bathsheba:* The widow of Uriah, a non-Jew who had risen to prominence in King David's army. While Uriah was out on duty, David ordered Bathsheba to the palace and slept with her. When he discovered she was pregnant, David had Uriah killed so that he could marry her. Their son Solomon succeeded David as king.

The genealogy of Jesus, the descendant of Abraham, is therefore a "mixed" one that includes both Israelites and non-Israelites, saints and sinners.

Two other surprises come in the final third of the genealogy. First, although Matthew says there are fourteen generations (Matthew 1:17), he only names thirteen generations in this section. Perhaps he was counting both Joseph and Mary in his enumeration. More surprising is that this Jesus' genealogy is mediated through Joseph, not through Mary, even though Matthew says that Jesus' conception was "from the Holy Spirit"

(1:18, 20)! Joseph is the one who provides for Jesus his identity as "the son of David, the son of Abraham" (Matthew 1:1).

This is not all that Matthew tells us about Jesus' identity. In the second part of Matthew 1, we learn that Jesus is not only the son of Joseph and Mary, but also a divine child conceived by the Holy Spirit (verse 18). As the one who would "save the people from their sins," he was to be called "Emmanuel"—God with us (verse 23). Here too, Joseph was no idle bystander in the miracle of the incarnation. Joseph's faithful participation was central.

Matthew 1:18-25 reveals that Joseph was a just man who faithfully obeyed the Law of Moses. He was also compassionate, not wanting to expose Mary to public disgrace (verse 19). In his obedience, Joseph was also no slave to tradition and right appearances; he was ready to respond to God's startling Word when it came to him in a dream. Despite the stigma, Joseph moved forward in his original plan to marry his bride. He also decided to accept Mary's child as his own legal heir, naming him Jesus.

It's not the secular world that presents me with problems about Christmas, it's God.

Cribb'd, cabined, and confined within the contours of a human infant. The infinite defined by the finite? The Creator of life thirsty and abandoned? Why would he do such a thing? Aren't there easier and better ways of God to redeem his fallen creatures?

And what good did it all do? The heart of [humanity] is still evil. Wars grow more terrible with each generation. The earth daily becomes more depleted by human greed. God came to save us and we thank him by producing bigger and better battlefields and slums and insane asylums.

And yet Christmas is still for me a time of hope, of hope for the courage to love and accept love, a time when I can forget that my Christology is extremely shaky and can rejoice in God's love through love of family and friends.

—Madeleine L'Engle

In this first story of the New Testament, therefore, we are presented with something of a mystery. God's salvation of the world—both Jews and Gentiles—is the work of God. Yet, as the involvement of Joseph shows, God nevertheless uses obedient human responses to help accomplish that miracle.

Things to think about: The nativity stories are about God's surprising intervention in human history. What are some ways that God has clearly intervened in your life? What was your role? Would God's work have been accomplished without your involvement? In what sense do we claim that God alone brings salvation?

What do you know about your genealogy? Who are some of the key figures in your family tree? What patterns do you see of God's intervention and human faithfulness?

PART II: SESSION

FOCUS (10 MINUTES)

Divide into two groups. On a sheet of newsprint or a chalkboard, Group A prepares a list of arguments that support the following statement: *God helps those who help themselves.* Group B prepares a list of items that support the statement: *Just trust the Lord.* Allow 8-10 minutes to prepare your lists. Reassemble as a large group and share your lists, then discuss:

How would you define the essence of the Christian life? Is it primarily about living according to God's revealed will in the Scriptures? Or is it primarily about God breaking into our lives in surprising, undeserved ways?

Transition: Joseph is often the forgotten character in the Christmas story, but his actions in today's Scripture show us a lot about human responsiveness to God in working out God's purposes in the world.

Forgetting nothing and believing all,
You must behave as if this were not strange at all.
Without a change in look or word,
You both must act exactly as before;
Joseph and Mary shall be man and wife
Just as if nothing had occurred.
There is one World of Nature and one Life;
Sin fractures the Vision, not the Fact; for
The Exceptional is always usual
And the Usual exceptional.
To choose what is difficult all one's days
As if it were easy, that is faith. Joseph, praise.

—W. H. Auden

Engage the Text (20 MINUTES)

Read Matthew 1:18-25 aloud. As a large group, make a list of all the items in these verses that emphasize Joseph's faithfulness. Then list all the items that emphasize God's surprising interventions. List these items in two columns on newsprint or the chalkboard.

Discuss: What does it mean that Joseph was a "righteous man" and why was it important for Matthew to emphasize this about Joseph (Matt. 1:19)? How did Joseph obey the angel's commission (Matt. 1:24)? What would have happened if he hadn't?

Now turn to Matthew 1:1-17 in order to see the "family tree" that Matthew draws for Jesus. What unusual features do you see? By including the genealogy, what is Matthew saying about the way God works in the world? What might it say about the human dimension of God's work of salvation?

Optional: In pairs, take two lumps of different-colored play dough or modeling clay, one representing God's intervention, the other representing human responsiveness. Create an image that illustrates the way God's intervention interacts with human responsiveness in bringing about salvation, healing, and hope in our world. In the larger group, share why you created your image.

Respond (10 MINUTES)

In pairs, share ways that you have been faithful to God, as Joseph was. These need not be heroic actions—just responses that you knew to be in line with what God has wanted you to do. As one partner reflects aloud about his or her faithfulness, the other makes a list of "(My Friend's) Faithfulness." Then trade roles and repeat the exercise. In a second round of interviews, share how God has intervened in surprising ways, despite failures and unfaithfulness. Here, the heading will be "God's Intervention in (My Friend's) Life." When you are through, discuss briefly the following question: "Which response to God is more difficult for you: obeying God's written word or accepting God's surprising interventions?"

Closing (5 MINUTES)

In a large circle, pray for the partner you had in Respond. If it fits with your group's character, leave some time open for participants to name some of the items from the lists, "(My Friend's) Faithfulness" and "God's Intervention in (My Friend's) Life." As a final benediction, hand your lists back to your friend with the words: "(Name), may God bless your faithfulness. May God surprise you. Amen."

PART III: LEADER GUIDELINES

Items Needed
Newsprint and markers
Paper and pencils or pens
Play dough or modeling clay
Bibles with Old Testaments

Resources
The following books may be useful for extra background on the texts used in this unit:

Brown, Raymond. *The Birth of the Messiah.* New York: Doubleday, 1993.

Fitzmyer, Joseph A. *Luke* in the Anchor Bible Series. New York: Doubleday, 1981.

Gardner, Richard. *Matthew* in the Believers' Bible Commentary Series. Scottdale: Herald Press, 1991.

Tips for Leading

1. You may want to contact someone prior to the class and ask them to be prepared to read Matthew 1:18-25 aloud.

2. In the Engage the Text section, at the end of the discussion of Matthew 1:18-25, be sure the group understands that Joseph's obedience was crucial, because it established Jesus' genealogical line, linking him to the fulfillment of God's promises to the people of Israel. It might be helpful, before your session, to draw up a chart of Jesus' genealogy as outlined by Matthew.

   Conclude the Engage section by pointing out that Joseph's genealogy includes four unusual names: Tamar, Rahab, Ruth, and Bathsheba. (See Matthew 1:3-6, and the Study section.) Say something like: "Matthew surprisingly includes four Gentile women in Joseph's and Jesus' family tree. Joseph's genealogy emphasized both his family's faithfulness and God's surprising intervention in including the Gentiles as part of God's work among Israel." If you have time, your group may wish to read the stories of the unconventional members of Joseph's family tree: Tamar (Genesis 38), Rahab (Joshua 2), Ruth, and Bathsheba, the wife of Uriah (2 Samuel 11).

3. If you are using this unit during the Advent season, consider setting up an Advent wreath and candles as a worship focus for this and future sessions. As part of your opening or closing, you may want to sing Advent carols that relate to the themes of the sessions.

Session 2
Tender Mercies: Yesterday and Tomorrow

PART I: PREPARATION

Bible passage: Luke 1:5-25, 57-80

Key verse: "And you, child, will be called the prophet of the Most High; for you will go before the Lord to prepare his ways, to give knowledge of salvation to his people by the forgiveness of their sins. By the tender mercy of our God, the dawn from on high will break upon us, to give light to those who sit in darkness and in the shadow of death, to guide our feet into the way of peace." (Luke 1:76-79).

Summary: In John the Baptist, the child promised to Zechariah and Elizabeth, the history and the hopes of the people of Israel begin to reach fulfillment. How do our past experiences with God and God's people enable us to expect new tender mercies from God in the future? How does our history help us see paths of peace for tomorrow?

> Gabriel is one of the two angels named in the Hebrew Bible (Dan. 8:16; 9:21), the other being Michael (Dan. 10:13, 21; 12:1). Along with Michael, Gabriel regularly figures as one of the four archangels [in other Hebrew literature]...The positioning of the four archangels around the throne of God or other sacred space has a long subsequent history in both Jewish and Christian tradition.
>
> —Carol Newsom, *Anchor Bible Dictionary*

Study: Luke's Gospel opens with the birth of John the Baptist. At the beginning of the story neither Zechariah nor Elizabeth anticipate having children, since they are well past childbearing age. In their day, as in many cultures today, Elizabeth's barrenness would have carried a huge stigma. Childlessness was seen by many as a sign of divine displeasure, while abundance of children was understood to be a divine blessing. (See I Samuel 1: 6, 7; and Psalm 127: 3-5, for example.)

We are told, nevertheless, that Zechariah serves regularly as a priest in the temple in Jerusalem. One day when Zechariah is fulfilling his priestly duties, the angel Gabriel appears to him and announces to him that his wife Elizabeth will bear him a son.

This story illustrates well how the Gospel writers reflect themes and narratives from the Old Testament in telling the story of Jesus. Here, two such stories help illuminate the birth of John the Baptist. The first is the story of another older and barren couple, Abraham and Sarah, who are also promised a child and descendants (see Genesis 15:1-6; 17:1-17; and 18:1-15). In the biblical record, conception and birth are seen as acts of God. It is God who opens the womb and God who enables birth to happen. But these stories of conception and birth are not simply miracles giving evidence of an almighty God. In every instance, when God promises a child to a barren couple, God lays a claim on the future of the child.

Luke 1:68-79 is referred to in the historical liturgy of the church as the *Benedictus*. This text is one of the four canticles, or "little songs" that is most used in Christian worship throughout the centuries. The other three primary canticles are the *Benedicite* (vv. 35-66a of the Song of the Three Holy Children in the Apocrypha), the Nunc Dimittis (Luke 2:29-32), and the *Magnificat* (Luke 1:46-55).

—New Westminster Dictionary of Liturgy and Worship

The child of promise is to play a crucial role in God's plan. So it was with Isaac, the son of Abraham and Sarah. And so it will be with the son of Zechariah and Elizabeth.

The second Old Testament narrative that informs about Luke's story is Daniel 9:20-27. This text not only gives us some clues as to the role that John will play in God's plan, it also provides backdrop for the appearance of the angel Gabriel to Zechariah:

"While I was speaking, and was praying and confessing my sin and the sin of my people Israel, and presenting my supplication before the Lord my God on behalf of the holy mountain of my God —while I was speaking in prayer, the man Gabriel, whom I had seen before in a vision, came to me in swift flight at the time of the evening sacrifice. He came and said to me, "Daniel, I have now come out to give you wisdom and understanding. At the beginning of your supplications a word went out, and I have come to declare it, for you are greatly beloved. So consider the word and understand the vision." (Dan. 9:20-23)

The appearance of the angel Gabriel to Zechariah while he is in the temple recalls this vision of Daniel's. The fact that it is Gabriel who announces the birth of John suggests that the announcement carries a message of great importance for all of God's people. The expectation of this child, whom Zechariah will name John, is that he will prepare the way for another, greater reality. His role in God's plan will be "to make ready a people prepared for the Lord" (Luke 1:17).

Zechariah reacts to Gabriel's announcement with an appropriate astonishment. "How shall I know this?" Gabriel's response in making Zechariah mute seems harsh to us. But the muteness of Zechariah during the months of Elizabeth's pregnancy shows that he has, indeed, had a divine encounter. His muteness also enables Luke to accent the astonishment of Zechariah's and Elizabeth's neighbors when Zechariah and Elizabeth both declare independently that the child's name is to be John (see Luke 1:57-66). The crowd, amazed at the naming of John and the simultaneous healing of Zechariah, ask, "What then will this child be?" Zechariah's first words after the long months of silence consist of a prophetic benediction, known in Christian tradition as the *Benedictus*.

This song is a lyrical summary of Israel's experience of relationship with God. Zechariah blesses God for having maintained the promise that he gave to David (see 2 Samuel 7) and before David to Abraham (see Genesis 12:1-3). Through this covenant God had displayed tender mercy, opening up barren wombs, intervening on behalf of God's people. Throughout Israel's history together—including the times when the people had been unfaithful, God had been faithful. In response, the people Israel were called to serve their God in holiness and righteousness. Zechariah's and Elizabeth's son John will prepare the way for the salvation that God will bring to all those who live in darkness. God's tender mercies and faithfulness continue. Likewise, Zechariah's song and his son continue to call God's people to follow the way of peace.

> Mistakenly, Tradition is often thought of as words, rules, or doctrines handed on or handed over. But in a strange paradox this is not actually its meaning. For no such thing as 'tradition' exists to be handed over. Rather, it is the action of handing on and handing over that is the tradition. Tradition is the process by which humans communicate ways of knowing, ways of being, ways of doing from one generation to the next. Tradition is the handing on of life and of living...
>
> —Maria Harris

13

Things to think about: Reflect on the ways God has acted in your life and in the life of your community in the past. You may wish to ask one of your friends or family members to tell you about a time when God has acted in his or her life. Do you expect God to continue to act towards you in merciful ways? Why or why not?

How have God's actions in the past led you into peaceful ways of living rather than contentious and distrustful ways? Where do you and your community need peace today?

PART II: SESSION

Focus (7 MINUTES)

Divide into two groups: optimists and pessimists. The pessimists will brainstorm a list of historic events that tend to lead us to despair and hopelessness. The optimists will brainstorm a list of events that give us reason to hope. Repeat the exercise, listing events in biblical history—with the pessimists listing stories in the Bible which seem to produce cynicism and hopelessness, and the optimists listing stories in the Bible which give hope. Put your lists of events on newsprint and post them prominently.

Transition: Just as the important people and landmarks in our history give us inspiration and meaning as we go into the future, so the history of God's people gives meaning and force to the stories around the birth of Jesus, including the birth of Jesus' forerunner, John the Baptist.

Engage the Text (18 MINUTES)

Luke's narration of the annunciation and birth of John the Baptist (Luke 1:5-25, 57-80) seems to echo parts of stories and prophecies of the Old Testament. In order to understand the significance of the story in Luke, it helps to look into the background material in the Old Testament.

Divide into three groups. Each group will investigate one key Old Testament story or prophet to see how Luke has used that Old Testament material in narrating the story of Zechariah and Elizabeth. Following your discussion, prepare to reassemble in the large group by appointing one person to retell the Luke story, and one to explain what parallels you found in the Old Testament.

Group A: Read Luke 1:5-25 and Genesis 17:15-21; 18:9-15. What similarities and differences do you notice as you compare Gabriel's announcement to Zechariah, and God's promise of a son to Abraham and Sarah?

Group B: Read Luke 1:5-25 and Daniel 8:15-27; 9:20-22; 10:1-19. What similarities and differences do you notice as you compare Zechariah's experience in the temple with Daniel's visions of God?

Group C: Read Luke 1:5-25 and Judges 13:4-5; 1 Samuel 1:9-15; and Malachi 3:1-4. How do the stories of Samson and Samuel and the prophecy of Malachi compare with the promise that Gabriel gives about John the Baptist in Luke 1:14-17?

When ready (10-12 minutes), reassemble in the large group and retell the story of John's birth, complete with explanations of what you found in the Old Testament passages. Then discuss: What purpose do you see in the apparent similarities between these Old Testament passages and Luke's narrative? What significance do the Old Testament passages give to the birth of John?

Listen to a group member read Zechariah's hymn of praise in Luke 1:67-79. As he or she reads, write your answer to the question of Zechariah's and Elizabeth's neighbors in Luke 1:66: "What will this child be?"

Respond (15 MINUTES)

Option 1: Get into groups of two or four, with equal representation of "pessimists" and "optimists" from the Focus activity. Discuss: In your lists of historical events, were there more stories of despair or more of hope? In the list of biblical stories, did the hope stories or the despair stories prevail? What difference does a faith story make in your outlook on the future?

As a group, pick a situation close to home—in your church, family, or community—that you feel needs an infusion of hope. What biblical stories of hope would be relevant to that situation? Or what stories of hope from your own experiences would help to awaken an awareness of God's good news? Write down a way that you can become an agent of hope in the coming week.

Option 2: Role Play. Depending on your time available, choose members of the group to role-play one or both of the following situations.

a) An unwed mother, rejected by her family and living on welfare, approaches a Christian at a bus stop. The mother asks the Christian for spare change. The Christian, knowing that the woman is looking for help, responds with an offer of help, and with a story of comfort.

b) An older church member feels the church of today is going to pot. This member focuses on tales of human weakness and woe. Another, younger church member feels the opposite, and tells stories of the church's resilience in history and dynamism, even today. A third member doesn't care, and says so in his or her comments.

Discuss: For those who role-played: What were your feelings as you played these roles? For those who observed: Which players did you identify with, and why?

Closing (5 MINUTES)
Stand to read Zechariah's song antiphonally, with half of the group on one side of the room and the other half on the other side. When you have completed reading the hymn, say "Thanks be to God!" and dismiss the class.

Option: If you do not have access to the same translation of Luke 1:68-79, two individuals can read the song antiphonally. The entire class can respond to the reading with the phrase "Thanks be to God!"

PART III: LEADER GUIDELINES

Items Needed
Chalkboard and chalk, or newsprint and markers
Tape to attach the newsprint to the walls
Enough Bibles for everyone to have one; preferably (for the Closing) in
  the same translation

Resources
1. Read the following biblical passages in preparation for the Engage the Text section:

Genesis 17:15-21; 18:9-15
Daniel 8:15-27; 9:20-22; 10:1-19
Judges 13:4-5
1 Samuel 1:9-15
Malachi 3;1-4

Tips for Leading
In the Focus activity, it is best to allow those who are naturally pessimistic to join the pessimist group, and those who lean toward optimism to join the optimist group. However, if the groups are not balanced in number, suggest that some people move to the opposite group, even if they need to step out of their natural tendencies toward optimism or pessimism.

For Response Option 2, recognize that with any role-playing, there may be some awkwardness at first. Allowing a role-play to continue for at least three to five minutes lets people get over the awkwardness and begin playing the part. Allow this to happen, even if it means uncomfortable periods of silence. After all, that happens in normal conversation, too. Then remember to include a debriefing period afterwards, in which actors and observers alike can reflect on feelings during the role-play.

Session 3
Vigorous Submission

■

PART 1: PREPERATION

Bible passage: Luke 1:26-56

Key verse: "Here am I, the servant of the Lord; let it be with me according to your word." (Luke 1:38)

Summary: Mary exemplifies the true nature of discipleship. Her patient submission to God's Spirit propels her into an active praise of God. Can submission lead us to vigorous action? How can we understand submission as a positive and energizing characteristic of faith?

Study: Gabriel announces to Mary that she will bear a child who will fulfill the role of God's Son in delivering God's people from sin and oppression. The familiar story sets the stage for the remainder of the Gospel. In Jesus, God has come to establish God's reign among humanity. However, this story tells us not only about how God acts through this Son; it also describes for us how the true disciple, however ordinary, responds to the call of God.

Luke 1:26-56 can be divided into two major sections. The first part of the passage, Luke 1:26-37, narrates the announcement of Gabriel to Mary. The second part, Luke 1:39-56, describes the response of Mary and of her cousin Elizabeth to the angel's announcement. At the pivotal point between these two major sections lies the central affirmation of Mary in response to Gabriel, "Here am I, the servant of the Lord; let it be with me according to your word."

Luke's narration of Gabriel's announcement to Mary follows the pattern of other biblical appearances of angels. Compare, for instance, the narrative of Gabriel's announcement to Mary with Gabriel's announcement to Zechariah:

1. Gabriel appears (1:11, 1:26-28)
2. Zechariah/Mary is startled (1:12, 1:29)
3. Gabriel says, "Fear not" (1:13, 1:30)
4. Gabriel's message (1:13-17, 1:31-33)
5. Zechariah/Mary ask, "How can this be?" (1:18, 1:34)
6. Gabriel's response (1:19, 1:35)
7. The sign (1:20, 1:36)
8. Conclusion (1:22-23, 1:38)

Both Zechariah and Mary demonstrate the appropriate response to a visit from an angel. First, they are startled and afraid. The presence of God is no light matter, and the faithful rightly respond with awe. Not surprisingly, the first words of the angel are words of reassurance: "Fear not." God's messengers attend to the need for human reassurance. After the initial message of Gabriel, both Zechariah and Mary respond with confusion: How can this be? Or, How shall I know? Again, the angel responds with the necessary words of assurance, this time providing a sign that God's Word can be trusted. In the case of Zechariah, the sign given is his muteness. Gabriel's sign to Mary is that of Elizabeth's pregnancy. Mary surely knew that Elizabeth was barren, so her pregnancy at such a late stage of life would come as an effective sign that "with God nothing will be impossible" (Luke 1:37).

> "Spaciousness is always a beginning, a possibility, a potential, a capacity for birth. Space exists not in order to be filled but to create. In space, to the extent we can bear the truth of the way things are, we find the ever-beginning presence of love. Take the time, then; make the space. Seek it wherever you can find it, do it however you can. The manner does not matter, the experience you have there is of secondary importance. Seek the truth, not what is comfortable. Seek the real, not the easy."
>
> —Gerald G. May

The contrast between the announcements to Mary and to Zechariah lies in the difference between the energy of their concluding responses to Gabriel's words. Luke tells us simply that Zechariah "went to his home." Mary, by contrast, goes into action. Luke tells us that "Mary arose and went with haste" to see Elizabeth. Indeed, Elizabeth not only confirms for Mary what Gabriel had said about her own pregnancy, she exclaims with joy and blesses Mary. Elizabeth's benediction of Mary summarizes the essence of faithfulness and trust: "And blessed is she who believed that there would be a fulfillment of what was spoken to her by the Lord"

(Luke 1:45). That recognition by Elizabeth, in turn, spurs Mary on to proclaim her praise of God.

Luke 1:46-55, known as the *Magnificat*, is one of the best known hymns in Scripture. The song is an eloquent summary of how God brings salvation to the afflicted of the world. The hymn recalls the song that Hannah sang when she took her son Samuel to Shiloh so that he could serve the Lord (1 Samuel 2:1-10). Mary recognized that God's promise to her was in step with God's actions through history. God has always "helped his servant Israel" by exalting the lowly, providing for the hungry, and doing great things for those of low standing.

Mary's song is therefore not simply her response to the announcement of Gabriel to her, not merely a private exaltation, but also a proclamation for all time. Here lies the meaning of God's salvation. Here, too, lies the point of submission. God acts for the humble and the afflicted, and those who hear God's promise submit themselves to God's plan by involving themselves in God's saving work in the world.

Things to think about: One of the most difficult things in the world to do is to wait. Our world wants things done in an instant. This week notice the things that make you impatient. Why are you impatient?

Mary's response to Gabriel's message was to say simply, "Let it be to me according to your word." In many ways the experience of pregnancy is the epitome of waiting and submission. A pregnant woman submits to her need to care for a child who inhabits her body. She has no real control over this child or over when this child will be born. If you are a woman who has borne children, think about your own pregnancy and what you may have learned about submission and patience during your pregnancy. If you have never given birth, ask a woman close to you to describe her own experience of waiting and submitting to the unknown future housed in her own body.

PART II: SESSION

Focus (10-15 MINUTES)

How do you anticipate important events in your life? In groups of three or four, read through the following scenarios, and choose one with which you can identify. If you wish, add other scenarios of great events that you have anticipated.

1. You have just become engaged to be married to someone who has just signed on for a short stint of work overseas. You will be separated for

three months, then your fiancee/fiancé will be back for two weeks
before the wedding.
2. You have just received word that you have been promoted. It means
relocating to company headquarters across the country, in a different
climate than you are used to. You have talked it over with the family,
they have agreed, and you will be moving in six months.
3. Your teenage daughter has just won a national music competition, and
has been asked to be part of a tour through Europe and Russia. You
will be going as a parent chaperone. You leave in a month.

Share in the group what you are likely to do in anticipation of these
events. Are you patient or impatient? Does the waiting bring out the best
or the worst in you? Do you lie awake at
night imagining scenarios of how it will
turn out? Do you worry that the event
won't go as planned? Do you talk about it
with everyone you meet, do you host parties in celebration, or do you tend to be
low-key about it? Do you journal? Do you
plan well ahead, or do you like to leave
things to the last minute? After a few
minutes of sharing, reassemble in the
large group.

> Let nothing upset you,
> Let nothing frighten you.
> Everything is changing;
> God alone is changeless.
> Patience attains the goal.
> Who has God lacks nothing;
> God alone fills all her needs.
>
> —The "Bookmark Prayer" of Teresa of Avila

Transition: When the angel Gabriel announced to Mary that she would
give birth to Jesus, she began a period of waiting and joyful anticipation.
In our lives, when we wait for something to happen to us, we are no
longer in control. How can we turn impatience and anxiety into trusting
submission to the goodness of God?

Engage the Text (18-23 MINUTES)

As a group, create a chart in which you compare Gabriel's announcements to Zechariah and to Mary. For major headings, use the stages of
the announcement identified in the Study section (page 18). For each
stage, the parallel passages will be read aloud. After the passages are
read, discuss any differences you see between the two stories.

Now focus on Mary's experience in particular. Discuss: Why was Mary
frightened in this story? What in Gabriel's message might have alarmed
her? What words and actions in the story, both of the announcement and
of Mary's visit to Elizabeth, prompted Mary to gain courage and praise
God for the wonderful miracle occurring?

To answer the latter question, break into your smaller groups again. On sheets of paper, write out key statements—slogans or mottoes, if you will—spoken both by Elizabeth and Gabriel, and by Mary herself—that would have given Mary courage and joy as she anticipated an unknown future. Post the sayings around the room. It's okay if the same statements are repeated.

Respond (12-14 MINUTES)

Reflect quietly on the example of Mary's submission to God as the miracle of the nativity was being worked out in her. Examine the statements posted on the walls, and determine which message fits your situation best right now, as you anticipate the future. What is God is saying to you at this time of your life? Do you need:

- to hear the angel's word that with God nothing will be impossible?
- to respond to God in quiet acceptance of God's will?
- to bless a friend or family member who needs to be encouraged and affirmed in his or her faith?
- to praise God for salvation, healing, and hope in your life?

When you are ready, go to the worship center and write your saying on a strip of paper. Wrap the paper around one of the stones. During the coming week, this will be your reminder of your response to God's actions in your life. Carry it in your pocket or your purse.

Closing (5 MINUTES)

Conclude the session by singing one of the many song or hymn arrangements of the *Magnificat*, (Luke 1:46-55). Alternatively, read the *Magnificat* aloud together.

PART III: LEADER GUIDELINES

Items Needed

If you have not already established a small table as a worship center in your room, arrange such a table for this session
Blank sheets of paper, preferably of different colors
Pens and markers
Enough small rocks or marbles so that everyone in the group can have one
Several small slips of colored paper

Resources

1. Read the story of Samuel's birth to Hannah, and Hannah's song of praise in 1 Samuel 1-2.

2. Reread Luke 1:5-25 to refresh your memory about Gabriel's announcement to Zechariah.

Tips for Leading

Unless you choose the optional focus activity described below, place the marbles or stones, the strips of paper, and the pens on the small table before class.

The Engage the Text will go more smoothly if you prepare the chart beforehand, using the categories given in the Study section, page 18. During the discussion, make notes of comparison directly on the chart. Crucial comparison that you should comment on, if no one else does, is that Zecharias' response to the angel's announcement was somewhat passive (he went to his home), while Mary's was active: she went in haste to see Elizabeth.

For the latter part of Engage the Text, you want the group to discover the key messages themselves. But just in case they are missed, write the following on four sheets beforehand and have them ready to post:

Gabriel: "For with God nothing will be impossible."
Mary: "Behold I am the handmaid of the Lord; let it be to me according to your word."
Elizabeth: "Blessed is she who believed that there would be a fulfillment of what was spoken to her from the Lord."
Mary: "My soul magnifies the Lord, and my spirit rejoices in God my Savior."
Ask a member of the group to be prepared to read the *Magnificat* (Luke 1:46-55) at the end of the session.

Another Option for Focus:

Arrange with a member of the group ahead of time to arrive about five minutes late. Begin the session by explaining that you have asked another group member to assist you in leading today's session, but that the assisting group member has not yet arrived. Suggest that you and the group sit quietly while you wait on the group member to arrive. While you wait for the "late" group member you may either exhibit (a) a nervous impatience by looking at your watch and going frequently to the door to look out, or (b) a perfectly calm patience that ignores any nervousness of other group members. Choose which response you think will emphasize the group members' own impatience. Ask the "late" group member to bring in the materials needed for the Respond activity, and when he or she arrives to lay out these materials very carefully and slowly on a table at the center of the classroom. The "late" group member should be silent throughout this time. When the materials are displayed, the "late" group member may sit down and open his or her lesson or Bible, still without speaking.

Once this waiting period is over, ask the group whether they found it difficult to wait patiently for the "late" group member. Encourage some of the group members to share stories about times when they found it very difficult to wait. Ask: "Has waiting ever led you to rejoice?" Explain that the story of Gabriel's announcement to Mary illustrates for us the ideal of patient discipleship, but that it is sometimes difficult for us to understand how Mary's submission could lead to such easy praise.

Session 4
Heaven to Earth

■

Part I: Preparation

Bible passage: Luke 2:1-21

Key verse: "The shepherds returned, glorifying and praising God for all they had heard and seen, as it had been told them." (Luke 2:20)

Summary: The familiar story of the shepherds reminds us that the birth of Jesus brought a new order into the world. The angel's declaration to the shepherds that Christ was Lord challenged the rulership of Caesar and established a new peace on earth that was meant for all people. How does Christ's lordship challenge the order of our present world, especially in relation to my personal life and priorities? What peoples today are hungry for peace? What difference can Jesus' coming make in their situations?

Study: Luke concludes his narrative of the birth of Christ by telling us that the shepherds' report of the angelic announcement caused all who heard it to wonder. Mary, for her part, "treasured all these words and pondered them in her heart." (Luke 2:19). Now, some two thousand years later, is it possible for us to still wonder at these things, for us to ponder them in our hearts? Yet, that is precisely what this much-told story calls us to do.

The story begins simply: "When Quirinius was governor of Syria. . ." Luke wants us to understand that what he is about to tell us is something that happened right in the midst of ordinary human history. This story is more than simple history, however, for the city to which Joseph and Mary travel is the "city of David." Already we know that something special is going to happen, something that fulfills God's promise to David.

Mary gives birth. Amazingly, Luke's narrative is that stark: "And she gave birth to her firstborn son and wrapped him in bands of cloth, and laid him in a manger, because there was no place for them in the inn" (Luke 2:7). It is an ordinary birth. The celebration occurs elsewhere.

On a hill where common shepherds were watching their flock, an angel appears. As did Zechariah and Mary before them, these shepherds were filled with awe. Why would an angel come to *them*, who belonged to a marginal, despised occupation? The angel comforts them with the word, "Do not be afraid." The angel's message to the shepherds is that a great joy was going to descend upon all people. To verify their message, the angel tells the shepherds that they will find a newborn baby lying in a manger in Bethlehem.

Then the celebration begins. Luke writes that suddenly the whole court of God appears and begins praising God. But their adoration is not only of God "in the highest." The angels praise God because "on earth" God will bring peace among humans. The human and divine worlds are united in the song of the heavenly host.

But you, O Bethlehem of Ephrathah,
who are one of the little clans of Judah,
from you shall come forth for me
one who is true in Israel
whose origin is from of old,
from ancient days.

Therefore he shall give them up until the time
when she who is in labor has brought forth;
then the rest of his kindred shall return to the people of Israel.
And he shall stand and feed his flock
in the strength of the LORD,
in the majesty of the name of the LORD his God.
And they shall live secure, for now he shall be great
to the ends of the earth;
and he shall be the one of peace.

—Micah 5:2-5a

The shepherds respond to this heavenly celebration by saying to one another, "Let us go over to Bethlehem and see." When Mary was visited by an angel, the angel gave her a sign that her kinswoman Elizabeth was pregnant. And immediately, Mary "went to see." So, too, do the shepherds respond to the visitation by the angel by going "in haste" to see the sign of this great good news. As children eagerly tear into their packages on Christmas morning, so the shepherds hasten to see this gift that the angels have announced. When they arrive in Bethlehem and see that, indeed, it is just as the angel had announced, they tell everyone what the angel and the heavenly hosts had said, "To you is born a Savior, who is the Messiah, the Lord."

Two thousand years later it is difficult to respond to the shepherd's announcement with much astonishment. We know the story. We have in our homes figurines representing the characters. We have seen children act out the story, and some of us even remember that golden day in our own childhood when we ourselves got to play the role of Mary or Joseph. "Jesus Christ is Lord" is a commonplace, if meaningful, statement for us in our established Christian churches. But what about before? Before Christianity? Before the church?

"Jesus Christ is Lord!" The shepherds must have been mad. Was this what everyone wondered? Was this what Mary pondered in her heart. For, as Luke tells us at the beginning of this story, these were the days of Caesar Augustus, and everyone knew that Caesar Augustus was Lord. This great Caesar had brought peace to the Roman world—the great *Pax Romana*. War was at a minimum, new and better roads were built, the world was at peace…at least for those in power, for those who "mattered" in the Roman world.

This, then, is the astonishing reality announced by the shepherds: Christ is a different kind of Lord. This Lord unites heaven and earth. This Lord brings peace not only to the rich and powerful and to those who count in the public places of the world. This Lord brings peace to *all* people who respond in faith. This announcement that Jesus Christ is Lord, leads us to wonder. It encourages us to ponder the meaning of this peace for our time. But this announcement of God's act in bringing great joy to all moves us to "glorify and praise God" for all that we have seen and heard.

> Caesar was only one of the titles Augustus bore. Others were *rex, imperator, princeps, pontifex maximus* and so on. He ruled Rome and thus virtually the whole civilized world. He was worshipped as a god. People burned incense to him. Insofar as he is remembered at all, most people remember him mainly because at some point during his reign, in a rundown section of one of the more obscure imperial provinces, out behind a cheesy motel among cowflops and moldy hay, a child was born to a pair of up-country rubes you could have sold the Brooklyn Bridge to without even trying.
>
> —Frederick Buechner

Things to think about: What are your favorite memories of Luke's Christmas story? Do you remember acting out the story when you were a child? Do you have a favorite nativity scene? Which character or characters in the story would you most want to be if you were to act out the story today? Why?

Who are the shepherds of our society? Who are the powerful "Caesar Augustus" figures of our time? Who is it that we rely upon to bring peace in our world? "Ponder in your heart" the meaning of the angel's announcement: "Jesus Christ is Lord."

PART II: SESSION

Focus (10 MINUTES)

Imagine that you have just received a birth announcement from someone at work, or from a family member. This announcement is unlike any you have ever seen. In fact, it makes you angry, wondering, "How could someone put *that* on a birth announcement?" In pairs, create an outlandish birth announcement. It may be too boastful, or it may be directed towards an inappropriate audience. Give your imagination free reign.

Then pass your announcements around in the group. If you wish, vote on the most outrageous announcement.

Transition: Jesus' birth included a very unconventional birth announcement. Not only was it given to a group that was at the bottom of the prestige scale, it also made claims that through this baby, a new order had begun, and that it applied to all people on earth.

Engage the Text (20 MINUTES)

Read through the biblical passage for today. Count the verses that narrate the actual birth of Jesus, then the verses that tell the story of the shepherds. Which section is bigger? What does the size of the shepherds' story say about the importance of Jesus' birth announcement?

In sessions two and three we saw a pattern of events in the encounters between people and angels. In groups of three, flesh out the following outline of the angels' appearance to the shepherds (Luke 2:8-15), by adding a phrase or sentence for the heading. What do you notice is different between this account and the stories about the angel's appearances to Zechariah and Mary (Luke 1:8-23; 26-38)? (Clue: one of the standard elements is missing in the shepherds' story.)

The Setting:
The Appearance of the Angel:
The Response of the Human(s):
The Reassurance of the Angel: "Fear not"
The Angel's Message:
How can this be?
The Sign Given by the Angel:
Conclusion:
The Action of the Human(s) in Response:

As someone reads Luke 2:15-20 aloud, listen carefully for where in this account Luke emphasizes the human response of "wondering" and "pondering." What is it about the announcement that causes people to wonder?

Luke here is clearly emphasizing the announcement of the angel that Jesus is a Savior and that he is "Christ the Lord." What does it mean that Christ is Lord, rather than Caesar Augustus? Although we don't use "lordship" language in our society, what people or things call for our allegiance?

Respond (10 MINUTES)

Option 1: In pairs, create a new outlandish birth announcement, this time highlighting the birth of Jesus.

1. Fold a sheet of paper in half so that it looks like a card.
2. Look through one of the provided newspapers or magazines and find an article or a picture that illustrates the kind of person to whom Jesus can bring a new peace. Put this picture or article on the front of the card. This describes the *recipient* of the birth announcement.
3. Look through the newspaper again to find an illustration of an event that would be transformed in Jesus' rulership of the world. Put this picture or article on the inside of the card. This describes the *message* of the birth announcement. Write a saying beneath this picture that offers promise for peace.

When you are through, share your cards around the group. If you feel it is appropriate, pass your card on to someone who would be encouraged to receive it.

Option 2: Name some people and events that have really changed the world. Imagine what would have happened if they had not come along. Compare their accomplishments to those of Jesus. How do they differ, and how are they similar? How do the accomplishments of famous people become known? How do the accomplishments of Jesus become known? Discuss ways that we, like the shepherds, are called to announce the outrageous good news of Christ's birth.

Closing (5 MINUTES)

Close by singing either "Joy to the World" or "Angels We Have Heard on High."

PART III: LEADER GUIDELINES

Items Needed

Paper (preferably colored) and colored markers
Bibles
Copies of last week's daily newspapers, or recent news magazines
Tape or glue
Several pairs of scissors
Hymnals or Christmas carols

Tips for Leading

For the initial part of Engage the Text, you may wish to prepare a sheet of newsprint with the outline of a typical appearance of an angel in Luke.

In the discussion of the announcement, be prepared to highlight the fact that in this story of the angelic appearance, the shepherds do not ask, "How can this be?" It may be that this part is transposed to the final scene, where the shepherds announce the angel's message to the people, who are "amazed."

For the last part of Engage the Text, ask someone to be prepared to read Luke 2:15-20 aloud, slowly and meditatively, so that participants can reflect and jot notes as they listen.

Session 5
Sharing the Dream House

PART I: PREPARATION

Bible passage: Luke 2:22-40

Key verse: "For my eyes have seen your salvation, which you have prepared in the presence of all peoples, a light for revelation to the Gentiles and for glory to your people Israel" (Luke 2:30-32).

Summary: Faithfulness to the covenant with God enables Simeon and Anna to recognize God's new revelation in Jesus. Their joy in God's salvation makes them eager to share the covenant and the promise with everyone. How does our participation in Christian community help us recognize God's activity and anticipate God's salvation? Are we, like Anna, eager to share good news with everyone?

Study: Throughout his narrative about Jesus' birth and early years, Luke makes it clear that Jesus and his parents were faithful Jews who obeyed God's Law and believed in God's promises through the prophets. It is not surprising, then, that Luke tells us that Jesus' parents fulfilled their obligations under the Mosaic Law and made the appropriate sacrifice of purification following Jesus' birth.

Luke combines in this narrative two regulations in the Law of Moses: the purification of the mother and the redemption of the firstborn male (see Leviticus 12). Luke does not mention, however, that Mary and Joseph gave the five shekels required for redemption of the firstborn. This implies that Jesus is not so much redeemed according to Mosaic law, but presented at the Temple as a servant on behalf of Israel. As with other nativity stories, this one recalls, and is illuminated by, an Old Testament story: Hannah presenting the young Samuel to Eli at Shiloh (see 1 Samuel 1). Like Samuel, Jesus was presented for a special service to God's people.

Luke began his Christmas narrative with a story about a faithful man and woman, Zechariah and Elizabeth, who were associated with the temple. Now the story returns to the temple, where we encounter another faithful pair, Simeon and Anna. These elders declare their praises of God who has fulfilled the ancient promises in this one child, Jesus.

Three times in three short verses Luke indicates that Simeon is inspired by the Holy Spirit. Simeon is a "righteous and devout" man, which means he is a Law-observant Jew. He is "looking for the consolation of Israel," which means he is a Jew who anticipates the fulfillment of God's promises through the prophets. And he is waiting at the temple. These three—the Law, the prophets, and the temple —sum up the history of Israel's covenant with God. It is to this man, one who faithfully abides in Israel's covenant, that the Holy Spirit comes in inspiration. And so, seeing Jesus, Simeon immediately takes the child into his arms and praises God.

Declare his glory among the nations,
his marvelous works among all the peoples.
For great is the LORD, bless his name;
he is to be revered above all gods...
Say among the nations, "The LORD is king!
The world is firmly established; it shall
never be moved.
He will judge the nations with equity.

—Psalm 96: 3, 4, 10

Simeon's song of praise is known as the *Nunc Dimittis*. The theme of this canticle recapitulates the tones of the heavenly host when they announced Jesus' birth to the shepherds. Now that Simeon has seen "peace on earth" (Luke 2:14) in Jesus, he can "depart in peace" (Luke 2:29). Simeon's short song captures much of Israel's expectation of the Messiah as it began to develop during the Babylonian exile (6th century B.C.) and is recorded in chapters 40-55 of the prophet Isaiah. This great prophet of the exile proclaimed that God would restore Jerusalem, which had been destroyed by the Babylonians in 586-7 B.C.

The restoration of Jerusalem would, however, be a revelation of the glory of God not only for and to Israel. Through Jerusalem and Israel, God would bring salvation to the Gentiles. (See Isa. 40:5; 42:6; 46:13; 49:6; and 52:9-10.) Increasingly during and after the exile, Israel's prophets declared that Israel's God would redeem all of the peoples of the earth. Read, for example, Zechariah 2:10-11: "Lo, I come and will dwell in the midst of you, says the Lord. And many nations will join themselves to the Lord in that day and will be my people."

Simeon's song similarly highlights God's good news for all people. Yet the oracle that follows Simeon's song (Luke 2:34-35) indicates that in another sense, God's revelation to the Gentiles is not "good news" for everyone. The oracle foreshadows Jesus' own words to his disciples later in the Gospel: "Do you think that I have come to give peace on earth? No, I tell you, but rather division" (see Luke 12:51-53). As Luke will show in the opening episode of Jesus' ministry (see Luke 4:16-30), many in the synagogue will become irate that Jesus reveals God's intention to include the Gentiles in the salvation which had been promised to Israel. God's peace will cause some to stumble—not because God brings peace to Israel, but because God now includes the Gentiles along with Israel.

Luke summarizes this dramatic scene of the presentation of Jesus at the Temple through the simplicity of the faithfulness of an elderly prophetess named Anna. Her obedience and faithful prayers at the Temple "night and day" illustrate how faithfulness to the covenant with God prepares one for God's salvation: "She gave thanks to God, and spoke of him to all who were looking for the redemption of Jerusalem."

Things to think about: Simeon and Anna's readiness for the coming of Christ was rooted in their attachment to the temple and their deep identi-fication with God's people. How does involvement in Christian commu-nity help you recognize God's salvation in your world? Does your partic-ipation in church leave you satisfied or "always wanting more"?

In your Christian walk, do you expect bet-ter things just for yourself or for others, as well? In what ways do you hope for God's salvation for those who are "out-side" of the fellowship of God's people?

> And because of His visitation, we may no longer desire God as if He were lacking: our redemption is no longer a question of pursuit but of surrender to Him who is always and everywhere present. Therefore at every moment we pray that, following Him, we may depart from our anxiety into His peace.
>
> —W. H. Auden

PART II: SESSION

FOCUS (10 MINUTES)

In groups of two or three, describe to one another the house in which you currently live or a favorite house in which you lived in the past. How has this house shaped your life? What things have been possible in your life because you lived in this house? What things have not been possible?

After describing the homes in which you lived, imagine aloud with one another what a "dream house" would look like. You may wish to sketch this dream house on paper.

How is your idea of "dream house" determined by the houses in which you have already lived? (For example, a friend noted recently that she would someday like to have a house where the laundry room was next to the bedrooms; then she wouldn't have to carry clothes back and forth.)

Transition: The story of Jesus' presentation in the temple highlights two seniors, Simeon and Anna, who lived in and near the temple in Jerusalem. Their presence in the temple represents their faithfulness to Israel's covenant relationship with God. The covenant has been their "house," their home, even though it is not the final and perfect house for which Anna and Simeon and other Israelites have longed. Yet, they had lived faithfully in this house and could thus recognize, in Jesus, their "dream house" when they saw it. What prepares us for recognizing God's healing and hope when it comes breaking into our lives?

Engage the Text (20 MINUTES)

On a chalkboard or long strip of paper, write the following words across the top: Past, Present, and Future. Read the text in the following sections, with a different person reading each section aloud:

Luke 2:21-24
Luke 2:25-32
Luke 2:33-35
Luke 2:36-38

After each section, determine how the text speaks about the past, the present, and the future. List the responses under the appropriate heading. For example, in Luke 2:21 the circumcision of Jesus is discussed; this is a present action (in the time of the story). Luke 2:22 refers to the Law of Moses, so this is a past event or action.

After reading the text, discuss the following questions: In what ways were Simeon and Anna faithful to the covenant, the relationship between God and the people of Israel? How did their faithfulness to the covenant prepare them to recognize the salvation of God in the baby Jesus?

What would such faithfulness look like today? Who are the Simeons and Annas of your faith community? In what ways do they help you anticipate the new realities that God is trying to birth in your community? What are those new things to which God is calling you?

After Simeon sings his song about God's salvation, he pronounces a solemn oracle to Mary about Jesus' future. Find this oracle in the text and read it aloud. How is this oracle related to the salvation about which

Simeon sings? Why would the "revelation to the Gentiles" cause some in Israel to stumble?

Respond (10 minutes)

Return to the small groups with whom you shared your experience and fantasies of your "dream house." Imagine together what you would feel if someone came up to you and announced that your "dream house" had just been built and you could move into it next month! Now, imagine that upon arriving at your new dream house, you discover that it is indeed your dream come true, but someone has failed to inform you that the house is large enough for several families, and those families will be moving in with you. How does your "dream house" feel now? Is it still a "dream come true"?

Talk about ways to make your church more inclusive of others. What are the barriers to new people being accepted into the fellowship? What steps will your group make to take down the barriers?

Write down on a slip of paper a short list of the types of people with whom you would find it difficult to share the "dream house" of God's reign. Imagine turning over the extra set of keys to these people.

Closing (5 minutes)

In a few moments of silence, hold in your hands the list you made in Respond. Quietly pray for yourself and for individuals the list reminds you of. Pray that you may all look forward to sharing together in God's reign. Pray for courage and strength to share the good news with them.

As a closing benediction, read together the *Nunc Dimittis*, Simeon's prayer in Luke 2:29-32.

PART III: LEADER GUIDELINES

Items Needed

Chalkboard and chalk, or newsprint and markers
Paper, pencils and other drawing materials (optional for Focus)
At least four Bibles for those who will read the text
Slips of paper and pencils for each class member

Tips for Leading

For the focus activity, you might want to put up pictures of various kinds of houses around the room, or provide magazines for people to leaf through as they talk about the houses they dream about owning someday. Offer the drawing activity as an option for those who are inclined toward that activity.

For the respond activity, you may want to hint that inclusiveness of others in the church is indeed a question of ethnicity or race, but it is also much more. What implications are there for those who think differently on certain issues, or who may be of a different social class than you?

In preparation for the next session, draw attention to the Things To Think About activity on page 39.

Session 6
A Costly Salvation

◼

PART I: PREPARATION

Bible passage: Matthew 2:1-23

Key verse: "A voice was heard in Ramah, wailing and loud lamentation, Rachel weeping for her children; she refused to be consoled, because they are no more." (Matt 2:18)

Summary: Innocent children are slaughtered, and yet Jesus, the Prince of Peace, is protected. Why is salvation so costly? How are we to respond to violence in our world and in ourselves? What is the price of working for peace in our world? What will peace cost us?

Study: The second chapter of Matthew couples one of the most majestic narratives of Jesus' birth with one of the most troubling stories of the New Testament. We hear of wise men from the East who come to worship the newborn Jesus. But their homage to the baby who is said to be "king of the Jews" results in a mass slaughter of all the male children in Bethlehem. What are we to make of the majesty and honor, placed side by side with violence and hatred?

Christian churches traditionally celebrate the story of the wise men on the day of Epiphany (January 6). On this day we celebrate the way God's peace has come to the whole world. The wise men are foreigners—Gentiles—who recognize the kingship of Jesus. Yet, they are unable to find him on their own. The star, representing nature, is an insufficient guide by itself. They must stop in Jerusalem and consult the Jewish authorities in order to know where to find the new king. The chief priests and the scribes, after consulting the Scriptures, inform the wise men that the king will be found in Bethlehem. (See Micah 5:2 and 2 Samuel 5:2.)

When these Gentile sages arrive at the house where Mary and the child are staying, they rejoice and present the child gifts. These gifts of gold, frankincense, and myrrh, however, are more than just traditional birth gifts. They evoke the prophecy of Isaiah 60:6 that "all those from Sheba will come bringing gold and frankincense, and proclaiming the salvation of the Lord." (See also Ps. 72:10-11.) The salvation of the Lord has arrived and even the Gentile sages recognize it.

But the visit of the Gentile magi sets off a horrid chain of events. Herod the Great, who was king of Judea at the time, was a paranoid ruler, even slaying members of his own family in order to ensure his throne. When he heard that the wise men had received a revelation about a new "king of the Jews," Herod became enormously upset. He tried to trick the wise men into returning to Jerusalem in order to inform him of the child's whereabouts, but God warned the wise men to return by another route.

An angel also appeared to Joseph in a dream and warned him to flee to Egypt with Mary and Jesus. As Matthew points out in his quotation from Hosea 11:1 (Matt. 2:15), this sojourn in Egypt brings to mind the experience of the Israelites, who were liberated from slavery in Egypt to become God's holy people. The infant Jesus, therefore, is shown to be a new Moses, identifying with the larger salvation story of God's people.

Herod responds to this turn of events with uncontrolled rage, ordering all the boys two and under in Bethlehem to be killed. The quote from Jeremiah 31:15 (Matt. 2:18) is one of the starkest voices in the Gospels.

A Talmudic Tale:

In the Jewish Talmud there is a tale about the suffering of the Jewish people in the Babylonian Exile (6th c. B.C.) and how the major figures in Old Testament history pleaded with God in heaven to deliver his people. First Abraham pleads with God, then Isaac and Jacob. But God responds to none of these holy patriarchs. Then Moses pleads for God's mercy. When God turns a deaf ear to Moses, Moses then asks the prophet Jeremiah to join him in his mission of mercy on behalf of God's people in Babylon. Still, God does not respond.

Finally, Rachel, a matriarch of Israel, "leapt to the fray" and pleaded with the Holy One that he respond to his people. She reminds God how, although her sister Leah had deceived her and married her love Jacob, Rachel nevertheless refused to indulge in jealousy but continued to love her sister. "Surely," Rachel argued, "you, the creator and king of the universe cannot allow jealousy to keep you from loving your children!"

And God responded, "For Rachel I am going to bring the Israelites back to their land."

The passage refers to the experience of Israel when they were defeated by the Babylonian armies, wrenched away from their homeland and taken into exile. Like the Egypt experience, the Babylonian exile was a defining landmark in Israel's history as a nation. By referring to these great formative events, Matthew places the story of Jesus in the stream of God's saving actions in the history of Israel.

Our story, then, is one of tragedy and salvation interwoven together. The irony is stark: the Savior is saved, but Rachel's children die. Yet, this strange narrative reveals a strong truth about the nature of Jesus' kingship. As Simeon prophesied, Jesus would cause many to rise and fall (Luke 2:34-35). Matthew also recognizes at the very beginning of Jesus' story that Jesus' rule will cause division. On one hand, the Gentile wisemen recognize Jesus, along with faithful Jews like Joseph and Mary. On the other, the chief priests and the scribes whom the wise men consulted are those same officers who will consent to Jesus' death (see Matt. 16:21; 26:57). The political powers reject and fear this infant king. The birth of this king does not halt the violence. Babies are slaughtered. The goodness of God's kingdom clashes against persistent evil in the world.

Yet the story is not over. The angel will bring the child and his family "out of Egypt" (see Hosea 11:1 and Exodus 4:22) and God will manifest God's salvation to the world—both to faithful Jews and to wise Gentiles. Violence and fear are not the last word. God brings Jesus out of Egypt and into Galilee. From there— through his life, death, and resurrection, Jesus confronts the violent powers of darkness, and the peace of his reign rules in the end, despite the violence of the cross.

> "O God,
> Send thy freeing, inner peace to rescue us from the tensions that tempt us to snap back at loved ones.
>
> Send thy overflowing, enlightening peace to save us from the distance that separates us from those who should be friends.
>
> Send thy strengthening, warming peace to deliver us from the anxieties our nation seems to court in its preoccupation with secret wars and rumors of wars.
>
> Send thy cohesive, surrounding peace to free us from our need to dominate and control others.
>
> Help us to look within thy word, thy love, and our own soul's response to that love. Help us to know the things that make for peace. Amen.
>
> —Betty Jo Buckingham

Things to think about: As you read the newspapers this week, clip or tear out articles about situations where peace and salvation are needed.

You may select articles on war-torn countries, on some violent situation in your own country, or on some smaller incidents in your local community. As you read these articles try to imagine what might need to happen in order for peace to come into these situations. What will it cost in order for these people to know the peace and salvation promised in Jesus? Be sure to take your clippings with you to the session.

PART II: SESSION

Focus (10 MINUTES)

As you arrive, post your newspaper clippings at the designated area. This will be a focus for the prayer time.

Option 1: Write down four or five major conflicts that have happened in your life, in your community, or in the world as a whole. Write the first ones that come to mind. As a group, name the conflicts you have chosen, and classify them under two causes: fear and jealousy. You may wish to mark them on two sheets of newsprint or on the chalkboard. Then discuss:

Why does fear cause conflict?
What do you think people are most afraid of?
Why is jealousy an attitude that leads to conflict?
How can people rid themselves of fear and jealousy?

Option 2: Think of four or five of the most triumphant or happy events in your life, your church's life, or the world at large. Write down the first ones that come to mind. Then think about the costs that went into each. Whose loss was the gain of others? What financial sacrifices were made? What discipline was necessary?

Share your findings in the group. Then discuss: Does happiness ever come without sacrifice on someone's part? Does peace in the world come without risk and sacrifice?

Transition for both options: Although we often think of the Christmas story as being a gentle story about the birth of a baby who will bring peace on earth, the story of the wisemen confronts us with a violent incident in which Jesus is saved, but others are destroyed. What can we learn about the conflict in our world today from this violent story? What is the cost of peace?

Engage the Text (20 MINUTES)

Option 1: Acting out the nativity story has been a traditional way for children to engage it. Today we will act out the story of the wisemen once more so that we engage it from an adult perspective. Doing so may remind us of aspects of the story we may have forgotten or see something we didn't see as children. As you act, interpret the characters. Say what you imagine them to have said or felt.

a) The three wise men
b) Herod the Great
c) scribes and chief priests
d) Mary and Joseph
e) the neighbors of Mary and Joseph
f) the angel
g) the soldiers who killed the infants
h) parents of the infants who are killed
i) a narrator
j) the "voice of Scripture"

If you have a small group and cannot fill all these roles, break the story into the following scenes to allow the same person to play several roles:

Scene I: The Wise Men meet Herod (Matthew 2:1-8)
Scene II: The Wise Men Worship Jesus (Matthew 2:9-12)
Scene III: Joseph is Warned in a Dream (Matthew 2:13-15)
Scene IV: Herod is Enraged (Matthew 2:16-18)
If time is short, select either scenes I and IV or scenes II and IV.

Option 2: If some in your group are uncomfortable with acting, try a tableau version of the story. Reenact the story by having several people read the parts of the narrator and the characters, while others interpret the scene through miming.

Respond (5 MINUTES)
• Discuss: Soldiers, how did you feel about participating in the violent massacre of babies? For the others: What did you feel as you watched that scene?
• How can we identify with the fear and jealousy demonstrated by Herod?
• How do we need to lament, with Rachel, the violence that so often coincides with the advent of peace?
• What could we do or say to minister to the soldiers, Herod, or the mothers?

Closing (10 MINUTES)

Begin by sitting quietly, reflecting on the violence in our world and in our hearts. If you wish, quietly examine the clippings and the pictures that were brought to class. Think about the costs involved in bringing God's peace into a situation.

Either in groups or as individuals, compose three prayers for the session's closing: 1) a prayer of lament for those who have lost their lives or their livelihoods, or have otherwise suffered innocently, in the cause of God's kingdom; 2) a prayer of confession for the jealousy, hatred, and fear which lead to violent acts that try to thwart God's plan; 3) a prayer of intercession for the situations you identified in the clippings; and 4) a prayer of thanks for the relentless plan of God that brings peace to our hearts and peace to the world.

Option: Write the prayer that is most appropriate to your role in the play. 1) Lament: those who played the parents of children, their neighbors, along with the narrator and the scripture reader; 2) Confession: those who played Herod, the scribes, and the soldiers; 3) Intercession: the angel(s); and 4) Thanksgiving: the wisemen.

Gather again and say the prayers together. Then sing an Epiphany hymn, such as "Worship the Lord in the Beauty of Holiness," or "As With Gladness Men of Old."

PART III: LEADER GUIDELINES

Items Needed

Paper and pens or pencils

Chalkboard and chalk, or newsprint and markers

Props for the enactment of the story of the wise men and Herod (optional, but it would enhance the Engage the Text activity):

   robes

   crowns

   a makeshift scroll

   five to ten dolls

   a white sheet

   three colorful boxes

   swords

Tips for Leading

Prepare a bulletin board or some kind of visual center where participants can post their clippings or pictures from Things To Think About.

Anticipate that not all will have brought them. Find several yourself, and post them. These will become a prayer focus in your Closing.

For the Focus, Option A: Write the words "FEAR" and "JEALOUSY" in large letters on the chalkboard or on sheets of newsprint. After the group has written down their conflicts, invite them to name them, and list them under the headings. Some conflicts may go under both headings.

For Engage the Text, prepare a chart that lists the scenes of Matthew 2. If you wish, you might assign the various roles ahead of time for the enactment of the story. Be sure to reserve some roles for extra people.

The play acting is more meaningful if you arrange for props (see Items Needed). Either bring them yourself, or ask group members ahead of time to bring them. Be creative, and encourage the group to have fun in preparing for their scenes.
Since this is the last session of the unit, you may want to include a wrap-up prayer as part of the closing.